Everything You Need to Know Before Buying Your First Programming Book

Colby Sites

© 2014 Colby Sites

All rights reserved. No part of this publication may be reproduced, distributed, or transmitted in any form or by any means, including photocopying, recording, or other electronic or mechanical methods, without the prior written permission of the publisher, except in the case of brief quotations embodied in critical reviews and certain other noncommercial uses permitted by copyright law. For permission requests, write to the author at colby@gettingstartedwithapps.com

Although every precaution has been taken to verify the accuracy of the information contained herein, the author and publisher assume no responsibility for any errors or omissions. No liability is assumed for damages that may result from the use of information contained within.

Cover Design: Little Guy Logos
Editors: Michelle Moore, Sheri Sites, Sean Sapp, Joss Harrington, Dennis Chow, Casey Conner
ISBN: 978-1495295287
1. How To 2. Science & Technology
First Edition
Printed in USA

Contents

INTRODUCTION _____ 5

APP IDEAS _____ 7
    WHAT EXACTLY DOES THE APP DO? _____ 8
    CAN YOU IMAGINE OTHER PEOPLE USING YOUR APP? _____ 9
    HOW DOES THE APP DO WHAT IT NEEDS TO DO? _____ 10
    DO I HAVE THE EXPERTISE TO DO ALL THIS WORK? _____ 12
    HOW MUCH TIME WILL THIS PROJECT TAKE? _____ 13
    ARE THERE ANY LEGAL CONCERNS? _____ 14
    NOW WE'RE READY! _____ 15

PROGRAMMING LANGUAGE _____ 17
    JAVA — ANDROID _____ 19
    OBJECTIVE-C — IOS _____ 21
    XAML AND C# — WINDOWS PHONE 7/8 _____ 23
    BUT WAIT, THERE'S MORE! _____ 24
    GOING FORWARD _____ 29

CHOOSING A PLATFORM _____ 31
    INITIAL INVESTMENT _____ 31
    USER BASE _____ 34
    PAID VS. FREE _____ 36
    MONETIZATION _____ 38
    CERTAINTY OF RELEASE _____ 44
    CONCLUSIONS _____ 45

CASE STUDIES _____ 47
    APP IDEA _____ 47
    ANDROID _____ 49
    IOS _____ 61
    WINDOWS PHONE _____ 70
    PERSONAL PREFERENCE _____ 80

CONCLUSION _____ 81

GLOSSARY _____ 83

REFERENCES _____ 85

Introduction

I started writing apps in 2011 but had been interested in programming for mobile devices since at least two years prior. The multitude of decisions to make before even downloading the right software was overwhelming. Which platform should I pick? What app should I write? What language should I write it in, and do I need to buy a book on it? All of these questions made the process seem incredibly daunting. If I had just a little guidance, I could have made the plunge much earlier. So this book is dedicated to me circa 2009. You can do it!

If you came to this book looking for programming knowledge, you will be disappointed. Though this book contains code, I don't go into the fine details of programming. Instead, this book's intent it to teach you everything you'll need to know up until you pick up your first programming book. Imagine creating an app like making a meal. Learning to program is like practicing knife techniques and figuring out how to use your oven. Instead, this book is like a cookbook, showing you how to plan for the dish and use those tools to execute it.

I'm going to share with you what I've learned through experience and research about everything leading up to your first app. I'll show you the source code for my first app written for each major platform and give points on their pros and cons as well as the difficulties I had when programming. It should be noted that although I had programming experience before writing my apps, it was never more than cursory knowledge with each of these platforms. I still did my fair share of reading, internet searching, and trial and error to get my code to work. I'm sure you will too.

I'll also talk about advertising networks and give you platform statistics so you can decide where to start your app writing quest. You don't need to be a programmer, marketing guru, or **user experience** designer to get off to a good start. You don't even have to know all the terms. I'll define the most important ones, denoted by being bolded and underlined like user experience above, in the glossary. By the end of this book, I will demystify everything to come before you purchase your first "How to Program" book.

App Ideas

The first thing we'll need on our quest to start making **apps** is a solid idea. If you just want to dabble around with the languages and platforms to see what you can do and how, then go ahead and skip this section. But if you want to make a killer app, you've got to have a concrete idea — and no, "I want to make the next Instagram" won't cut it. Many questions need to be answered before you start considering platforms, languages, and models. Like any good building, before you construct it, you must architect it. In order to have a strong foundation for your app, come up with the core concepts behind it, followed by features adhering to the principles of the core, and lastly, add any frills to make the app nicer and enhance the features you've decided on. By setting up a solid foundation of ideas and axioms by which you design your app, you can make more objective decisions that aren't colored by personal preference. Think of the following graphic as the layers of your app, with ideas further away from the center being easier to change and less important to the app's foundation.

App Architecture

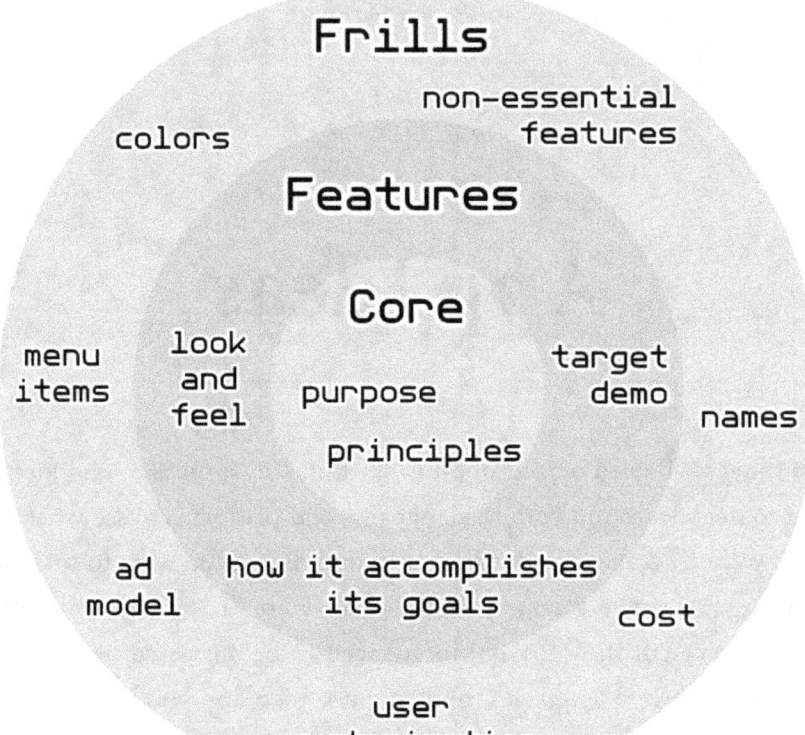

What exactly does the app do?

Determining what an app does is perhaps the most basic task when designing an app, and though it should be relatively straightforward, it is often the most difficult to settle on. Think of something in your life that could be made easier, a quick, fun activity you enjoy, or even a smartphone novelty. Maybe you'd like to check your stocks on the go. Perhaps you just want to recreate a cool Flash game you played when you got bored in the 90s. Or maybe customizing your phone's dialer is up your alley.

Whatever the case may be, all great apps are built on a foundation of solid ideas and principles adhering to a core concept. Come up with a set of requirements you want to hold to firmly, or ideas for the app that are important to you. These ideas can range from "I want to make a game about emphasizing clever puzzle solving above pretty graphics," to "I want to create the most user-friendly runner's app on the market." With these principles at your disposal, even if you are having a tough time making a decision related to the app, all you need to do is come back to the axioms you've laid out. Questions like "Should I include music?" or "I wonder if syncing this to my Facebook would be good?" are easily answered when you examine what your app is supposed to do, rather than what you would prefer. Answering these questions and settling upon a core idea leads into our next step.

Can you imagine other people using your app?

Now that you have an idea, can you see someone using your app? If you installed your program on a friend's phone, do you think they would use it? Do you think someone who doesn't know you would find your app appealing? Lastly, would you yourself use it?

Determining how marketable and useful your app is to someone will allow you to set your expectations accordingly. If you think the idea could be profitable and would fulfill a market need, try asking around to see if people would use it. When they give you feedback, make notes of it and consider altering your app to incorporate their suggestions.

Perhaps your app wouldn't appeal to everyone? There's nothing wrong with that, and there's something to be said for making an app just for you. The good thing about not expecting an audience is you can customize it to be exactly what you want and it doesn't have to be pretty. Making a quick and dirty app to get something you need done is just as valid as having a nice, polished app everyone can use.

If you think you'll get a return on your time invested, monetarily or otherwise, then it's now time to ask yourself the next logical question.

How does the app do what it needs to do?

I feel would-be app makers overlook this question most often. Knowing you want to check your bank account online is one thing, but planning how to do it is quite another. Since I'm a relatively tech savvy person and know how to program, I often get approached with app ideas by the people around me. They've thought up the pricing, what it should do, where to release it, new features to add, and websites on which to advertise, but when I ask for details on how to do it, they generally answer with "Oh, I have no idea!" Unfortunately, you can't get far with the where, when, and why of an idea, but not the how.

Arguably, answering the question of how the app functions is difficult when you have little to no knowledge or experience in the subject. However, I think breaking down an app idea into its basic components is the bare minimum requirement to begin work, and it doesn't take any experience in the field or prior programming knowledge.

Let's take the personal bank account idea as an example. It accesses your bank account online to get information, so that's one block you need to code. You'd also like to make it appealing and easy to use to users, so the **User Interface** (UI) is another consideration. So our system currently looks like this:

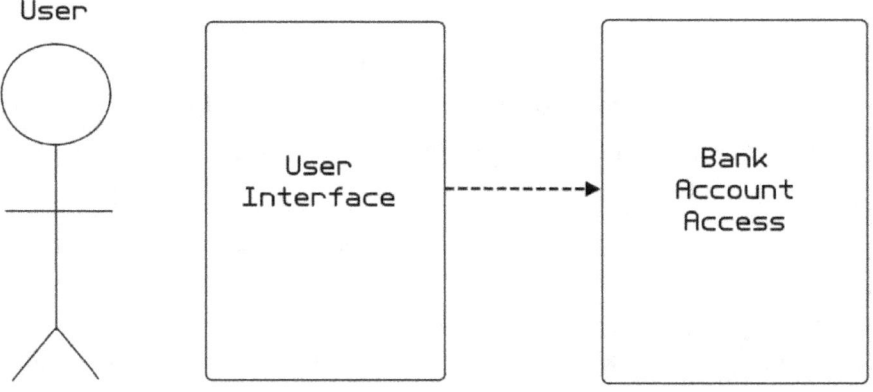

Now let's break these blocks down further. For the Bank Account Access block, we may want to keep a history of bank account information. It would be very user-friendly to allow people to save their information to the app so they don't have to re-enter it every time the app is opened. Let's not forget the critical task of this block — communicating with the online banking system and retrieving its data. The sensitivity of the data means all of these tasks need to be done safely and securely, as our users' privacy and securing their personal data should be a top priority.

For the UI, we'll want the user to be able to choose their settings for their bank account, such as displaying balance or the last three transactions. There should also be settings specifically for the app, like whether or not it retrieves data automatically, or how to display the information. Both of these settings should most likely be accessible from a menu. We'll also need images to make it look more professional and visually appealing. If we have bank account history, we may want to have a graph function show the data in a way the user can easily see. To put the icing on the cake, having a nice bit of **haptic feedback** (in the case of mobile phones, usually vibration) and audio cues makes the experience feel better to the user.

Now all of a sudden, our system looks like this:

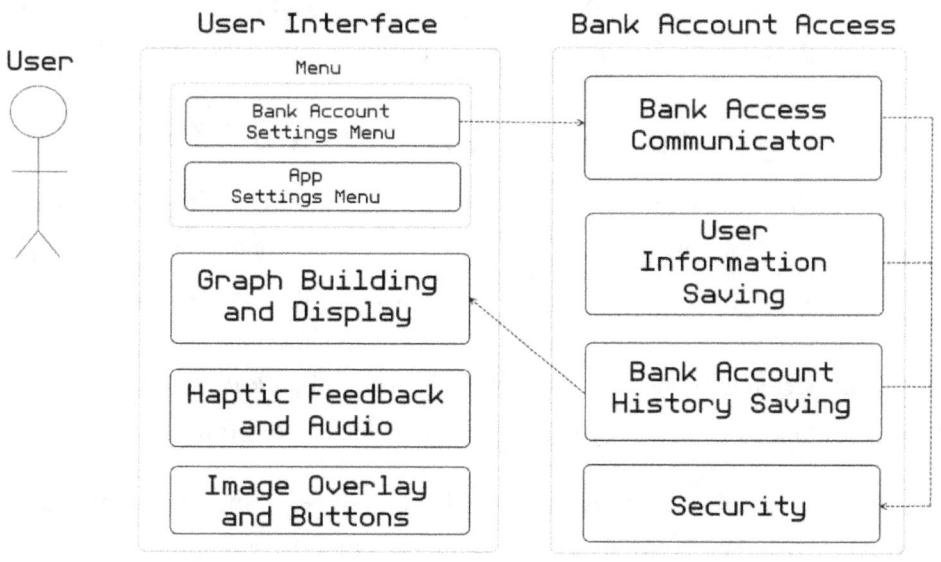

Looks daunting, doesn't it? Ah, the double edged sword of planning. It reveals the ugliness and scope of the work to be done, but it also forces you to think about the importance of your features and the manageability of the workload. If you're an experienced programmer, you can continue to break these blocks down according to how you want to code each feature. However, if you're a beginner this is more than enough information with which to continue planning.

From a diagram like the one above, you can start cutting features you think you won't need. Maybe you don't care about saving bank account history or graphing it. Perhaps it's enough to just display the current balance, which would mean even less information needing to be pulled in the Bank Access Communicator. It could be you think a bank account app has no need for audio cues. By removing features or frills you think don't add enough value or would be too difficult to add, your timeline and workload are reduced, increasing the likelihood that you'll finish your project on time.

Another important consideration is whether or not you can actually access the data you need. Some companies offer ways to query their website for data, while others keep such information private. If the bank you've decided to make the app around doesn't have a way to access the relevant information, you'll have to change banks, find a workaround, or scrap the idea entirely.

When you've cut the plan down to something manageable and decided on a preliminary feature set, it's time to think of the work required to finish the app.

Do I have the expertise to do all this work?

If you know how to program, are you experienced enough to take on this project? If you have no idea how to code, are you willing to take the time to learn? Questions like these are absolutely essential, and will help you finalize your feature set by making you think about the scope of the work. Keeping the scope of your project small not only helps in project planning, but can allow for more growth after its release, when you have more experience to draw on.

Answering these questions also has the benefit of revealing requirements you didn't know you had. In our bank account example, there are at least two areas requiring expertise beyond app programming — graphics and security. Though it may be more work than you anticipated to complete this app with these two new areas you'll have to cover, they're necessary to finish the project. At this point, you'll either have to learn how to do three jobs or find someone who can do them for you. I know if I was making this bank app, I'd trust a graphic artist and a security expert to do what they do best while I work on the app programming section.

Consultations/contractors don't have to be very expensive. From freelance websites like guru.com and 99designs.com to friends on social media, you can find someone who will do the job within your budget. In fact, I bet you know someone who's a decent artist and whose style you enjoy. And though it's rare, but maybe you're acquainted with someone else who took a security focused programming class or has a passing interest in cryptography. Granted, I'd make the tradeoff of someone who's good at napkin doodles for a security expert who specializes in encryption/decryption code, but I'm generalizing here.

Users want their data safe, and you don't want to be at the butt end of a giant user data leak. Companies pay hundreds of millions of dollars every year to keep their users' data secure and safe. It's a big deal. In fact, it's such a big deal, entire fields of study are dedicated to it. That's not to say graphics aren't important, but if you have unappealing pictures, nobody's life is ruined by identity fraud. According to a February 2013 study by Appthority, 79% of the top 50 free iOS and Android apps have privacy issues, including those from big names like PayPal and Apple (Appthority, 2013). No one is exempt from security concerns, which means staying vigilant and designing with security in mind upfront is important.

Once you've decided on how much work there is to do and how many people you need to do it, you're prepared to move to the next step.

How much time will this project take?

You've mostly answered this question with the previous sections, but it's worthwhile to apply numbers to the areas you can. If you know nothing about programming, you'll essentially only be able to plan how long it will take you to learn how to code, but it's still better than nothing. As you gain more knowledge about the scope of the work, you'll be able to more accurately define your app's timeline. I know between a full-time job, a social life, cooking dinner, cleaning house, and the rest of life's responsibilities it can be hard to justify working on an app. I've found, however, when I had a schedule and deadlines, I stuck to my plans and was able to work more often and more efficiently than when I told myself I'd work whenever I could.

Are there any legal concerns?

To save time, you may be tempted to use pre-written code when making your app. For example, if you found a nice piece of code to convert a song file from one type to another, you'll want to find out whether it can be legally used by you for free or if you have to pay to use it. Like most intellectual properties, source code comes with a variety of copyright protections, from none (public domain) to full protection, to something in-between. If your app became big enough, it would be a shame to be sued and have to pay damages for using 12 lines of code you didn't know were copyrighted.

Another interesting consideration is the formats implemented in your program and the processes used to get to those formats. Though they're not extremely common, formats like MP3 are copyright protected for both their decoding and encoding, meaning if you're doing either of those, you'll have to pay the format owners to do so.

In addition to the source code of the app, finding out the trademarks and copyrights of the name you're looking at for your app is a good idea. You should search the US Government's trademark system online to make sure you're not stepping on anyone's toes or getting yourself into legal hot water with your naming choice.

> You may also want to check available domain names to make sure your app's name is suitably unique. You wouldn't want someone else getting Google hits for your work.

Though wading through trademark databases, searching for licenses, and copyright checking aren't the most interesting or rewarding experiences, it's important to make sure you can legally sell your app without worrying someone can take you to in court.

Now we're ready!

By completing these sections, though you may not have realized it, you've architected your app. You have a strong foundation, features built on those ideas, and frills to make things nicer along with a timeline and knowledge of the resources needed to make it all happen.

Armed with a plan, a set of requirements, a team, an idea of how much work is involved, and having your legal bases covered, you'll have a much easier time keeping yourself on task and moving ahead. Any questions from here on can generally be answered by the data you've lined out in this section. Heck, I've seen production software with less **documentation** and thought put into it than what we've just done here. Now it's time to dive in to details. We have a high level overview of what our app is and what it's going to take, so the next logical step is to determine how we're going to program it.

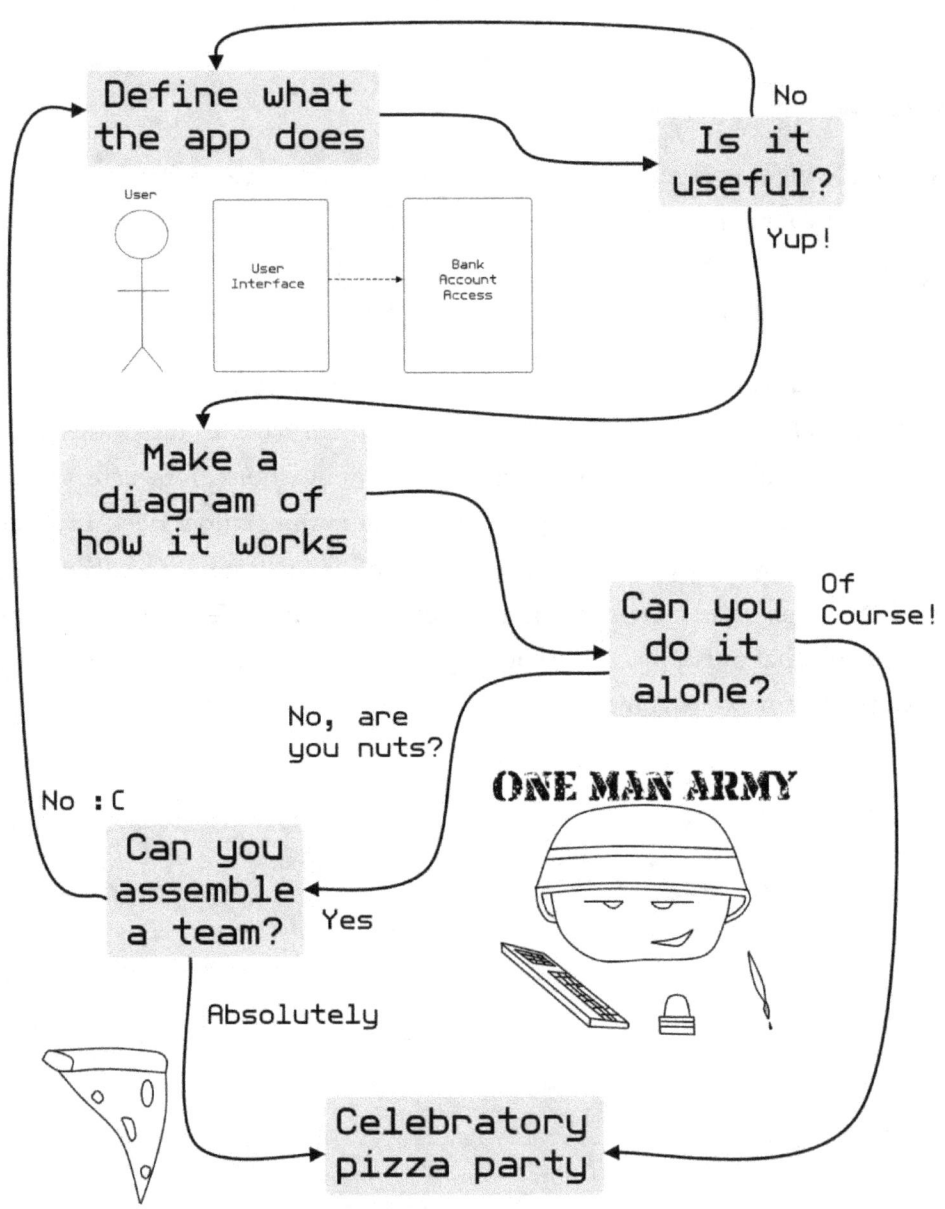

Programming Language

Though this section ties heavily into the next — choosing a platform — I believe it merits its own discussion. In a perfect world, you'd be able to write an app one time and release it for all platforms through a unified submission process and get paid through one entity. Unfortunately for all of us, that scenario is as far from reality as can be.

Each major platform has its own unique recommended language for programming. For Android, Java and XML are the languages of choice, iOS uses Objective-C, and for Windows Phone, it's a combination of XAML and C# (pronounced "C sharp"). These languages are not compatible with one another and you'll have to rewrite your code from scratch each time for every platform. There are a few multiplatform solutions to this problem, but we'll get into those later.

Each of the platforms also has their own **Application Programming Interfaces**, or APIs. These APIs are written by the maker of the OS, and are designed to provide programmers with functions to make app writing easier. So for instance, I don't have to write a function to write text to the phone's screen, there's an API which does it for me. These APIs make writing apps much faster and easier since most functions have already been written for you. You may want to investigate the security and efficiency of these APIs, even if they're from your app provider.

You don't want a well-designed and secure app compromised because you relied on someone else's code or used an untrusted API.

Every platform uses different APIs and you'll have to learn them as you learn to code in each language. Both parts are important, so I'll cover each of them as we move through the platforms. Before each section, I'll also include a "Hello World" example — a simple app just displaying the text "Hello World." This simple program should give you a feel for the code for each platform.

For a quick overview on each language, look at the summary box at the end of each section.

APIs and You

Imagine making an app like building a house...

Without APIs

You're making your own bricks. Though you know exactly what's going into them, it's time consuming and generally not worthwhile.

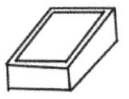

With APIs

You're using the bricks someone else made. You're not sure how they made them, and some may even be low quality, but as long as you trust the manufacturer, it will save you time and effort.

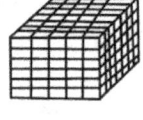

Using Game Engines

Instead of using bricks, you're using incredibly beautiful tiles someone made. Though they can't replace bricks, they can make things look much nicer for specific applications.

Conclusion

There's nothing wrong with buying bricks from someone if you don't want to take the time to make them yourself. Just make sure they're good quality, lest your house fall down.

Java and XML — Android

```
@Override
public void onCreate(Bundle savedInstanceState) {
    super.onCreate(savedInstanceState);

    TextView textView = new TextView(this);
    textView.setText("Hello World");

    setContentView(textView); }
```

Java is one of the world's most popular programming languages, and it's easy to see why. It's compatible with all systems, inherently **object**-oriented (meaning data is represented more like real world objects), and has easily implementable structures to get your code written quicker without having to worry about low-level programming concepts.

Java features large libraries of functions that make coding your algorithms easier by having pre-implemented code that you can use. These libraries allow for faster coding by taking away some tedious tasks you'd have to do yourself. Think of it like using a dishwasher instead of doing it by hand — it saves you time by eliminating tedious tasks. Overall, Java is a robust language and learning it will help if you ever plan on making multiplatform programs that aren't apps.

The programming may be done in Java, but most of the visual layouts are defined in XML, another industry standard language. It will look familiar to anyone who's done any amount of web programming as it bears a strong resemblance to HTML. However, XML is so customizable it's more pertinent to talk about its Android API than the actual language. The prebuilt structures provided to you by Google are relatively straightforward, though they do take time getting used to if you're not from a web design background. The documentation on the API is also quite extensive, which takes most of the confusion out of the process. Though you'll be working with the Android APIs and not pure XML, it'll impart a level of experience with the language you can reuse down the road.

To program using the tools provided by Google, you'll be using Eclipse, an **Integrated Development Environment** (IDE) that's also **open source**. It was first created in 2004, with its main focus being Java support, though it also handles other languages. Eclipse has some nice functions to make programming easier like an autocomplete feature to automatically pull up API calls and variable names. Its user interface is also easy to navigate once you get used to it. Like other IDEs, it features different views for different tasks (one view for programming and another for debugging), but the debugging window is less useful than I'd prefer. However, once I got used to the different views, it became easy to switch between them. Overall, the interface is semi-intuitive and powerful. Eclipse is also completely free, so you'll never have to pay for a license, and it's multiplatform so you're not tethered to one operating system to code on. If you're planning on learning more languages, Eclipse is an excellent platform on which to continue your programming education.

> **Pros:** *Java is used in industry and is inherently multiplatform. It also has a large library of built in functions. XML is industry standard. Eclipse is a great IDE and it's multiplatform.*
>
> **Cons:** *Views are sometimes difficult to get used to and debugging mode isn't as functional as other IDEs.*
>
> **Choose this if:** *You have any amount of Java experience or plan on using this language later on for PC programs.*

Objective-C — iOS

```
- (IBAction)showMessage
{
    UIAlertView *helloWorldAlert = [[UIAlertView alloc]
                                    initWithTitle:@"My First
App" message:@"Hello, World" delegate:nil
cancelButtonTitle:@"OK" otherButtonTitles:nil];

    [helloWorldAlert show];
}
```

Objective-C is the most obscure language on this list. Before iOS started using it for its apps, not only had I never used it, I had never even heard of it. Its obscurity is due to it being generally limited to UNIX and Apple platforms and I started coding on Windows.

If you have experience programming in any other language, Objective-C will be a bit of a trial to learn, or at least it was for me. Since it has the letter C in the name, I assumed it would be like other C and C derivative languages, but it's not. The language looks nothing like C and functions like it even less. Those issues may not be a problem if you haven't seen any other programming languages, but it was a jarring experience for me to switch to iPhone development from Android.

The upside to this radical language shift is it doesn't have to have the same pitfalls and ideas of the previously discussed choices. Variables can be dynamically typed, meaning there are no hard restrictions on what you can do with a variable. In Java, if you set a string variable to "7", you can't use that variable as a number because you've already said it's a string, a variable type that uses characters, not numbers. With Objective-C, you can use it as a number, a string, a character, or a Boolean, depending on what you need it to be.

The language also contains a useful message sending feature which allows communication with objects within the code. These messages allow for more flexibility when defining how an object in your code behaves not only with code you've written, but with other code you're using as well. In laymen's terms, message sending allows for more intuitive, flexible communication to objects in your code. You can also determine whether or not objects have specific traits with messaging, meaning your code can be more flexible depending on what kind of data you have. Objective-C is a quirky and interesting language with some advantages, though it can be confusing to programmers experienced in other languages.

XCode is the platform you'll be using for iOS development. It's developed and maintained by Apple and was originally released in 2003. Much like Eclipse, it also has its own autocomplete feature, but I found the UI less user-friendly. Trying to navigate options and menus to get the files I needed for my app left something to be desired. The difficulty I had may be due to my inexperience with Mac OSX, but I found the experience more frustrating than with other IDEs. The software comes bundled with OSX, meaning if you have a Mac, you've already got it, making it that much easier to start coding. Though it's not my choice of compilers, it's one of the best on the OSX operating system.

Pros: Object messaging, variable prototyping, and other features that set it apart from other languages. XCode comes bundled with OSX.

Cons: More difficult to read and interpret. Its usefulness is limited to Apple operating systems. XCode was less user-friendly in my experience.

Choose this if: iOS development is important to you and your future programming will be limited to Apple operating systems.

C# and XAML — Windows Phone 7/8

```
<Page.Resources>
        <common:BooleanToVisibilityConverter
        x:Key="BooleanToVisibilityConverter"/>
        <x:String x:Key="AppName">Hello, world!</x:String>
    </Style>
</Page.Resources>
```

C# is the next iterative improvement on C++, a programming language many institutions use to teach introduction to programming. Chances are if you've had a class on how to program, you've been exposed to this language's little brother at least once. The changes from C++ to C# are numerous, but the big picture is C# supports object-oriented programming more easily and takes care of some lower level functions C++ leaves up to the user.

In addition to being widely recognizable and having improvements over its predecessor, C# also interfaces with the .NET framework, a Microsoft-developed library which offers a multitude of useful functions helpful to newbies just starting out. Though Java has something similar, .NET has far more options to offer. Unfortunately, these libraries also have a small drawback. With so many functions and proprietary implementations of general programming structures, it can be difficult to pick up on and debug errors if you're not used to working with this platform. Before I became very familiar with it, I debugged many errors with their implementations simply because I thought they acted one way, but they did not. Fortunately, misunderstandings like this are quickly cleared up by Microsoft's extensive, free documentation for C# called MSDN.

The second component to the platform is XAML, a proprietary XML derivative designed by Microsoft (who saw that one coming?). This language looks very similar to XML, but it's used only for application layouts. In fact, every XAML file is compatible with XML, but not the other way around. The downside of XAML is it's quite unforgiving about syntax and the errors you'll get when programming are often cryptic. I once spent about two hours debugging an issue that turned out to be a misspelled name, something most other languages are quick to point out.

When using these languages for Windows Phone, you'll be programming in Microsoft's Visual Studio Express, a more lightweight, free version of their expensive professional IDE Visual Studio. The program has been around since 1997, so it's had time to grow and mature to a useful, intuitive platform. Like Eclipse and XCode, it also offers an autocomplete feature called IntelliSense, though I prefer it over the other two because it offers more in the way of information. Visual Studio Express also supports plugins for other languages, though they all function less well than those that are built-in. It's a nice platform to learn on because it's robust and free. Unfortunately, it comes with a caveat — you can't publish any of your code without buying a license. It's also a Windows exclusive piece of software, which may turn off some budding developers.

> **Pros:** C++ is a widely used language and C# is a small jump from there. .NET framework is helpful. XAML is powerful and straightforward. Visual Studio is a great development environment.
>
> **Cons:** .NET is almost too expansive. XAML isn't very good at telling you what's wrong.
>
> **Choose this if:** You have C++ experience or web programming experience.

But wait, there's more!

Programming in the previously mentioned platform-specific languages will generally squeeze the most **performance** out of your app. Alternatives to these single serving solutions exist, but their multiplatform capabilities often mean being slower than **native** apps. Here are a few of the most popular multiplatform app development solutions.

HTML5/CSS/JavaScript

```
<html>
        <header><title>This is the title</title></header>
        <body>
                Hello World
        </body>
</html>
```

As strange as it sounds, you can build rather powerful apps with the latest iteration of HTML, the language used to write most webpages. To be more precise, HTML5, CSS, and JavaScript all work in conjunction to create a fully functioning app with HTML5 defining the layout, CSS defining how it looks, and JavaScript powering the code. The combination of these languages provides a powerful platform for app developers looking to only write code once for multiple operating systems. In fact, up until August of 2012, Facebook used HTML5 as the basis for its mobile app.

HTML5 offers native video and audio embedding, as well as a powerful tool called **Canvas**. With Canvas, you can programmatically redraw images and shapes to a defined area on the screen, allowing for the display of games and more diverse interactivity with the user. Canvas is a general programming and display concept not specific to HTML5, but its inclusion in the webpage language really enhances the capabilities of the platform.

Since the app is defined by standards most web browsers interpret, it will be able to work on nearly any platform that has a browser, be it PC, Mac, Linux, or any mobile OS. The caveat to working with web browsers, though, is some may support certain functions the others don't. Just ask a web developer how long it took to make their website, then how long it took to make it compatible with Internet Explorer.

Once the main coding is done, there are programs that will make your website into a stand-alone app. The process is done by essentially making an app to open your webpage locally from the phone's storage space. A few programs exist to do this procedure automatically for you, the most popular being Phone Gap.

If you're looking to code a simple application and you don't want to manage multiple code-bases, making a web app with HTML5, CSS, and JavaScript is a great place to start.

> **Pros:** *Runs in any web browser, inherently multiplatform, can test on any system.*
>
> **Cons:** *Takes a performance hit since it's not native code, may have to debug browser-specific bugs.*
>
> **Choose this if:** *You have any web programming experience and your app idea does not require high performance.*

Unity (or other game engines)

```
using UnityEngine;
public class HelloWorld : MonoBehaviour {

    void Start() {
    Debug.Log("Hello World");
    }
}
```

If you want to code a game for the mobile platform space, game engines are the most enticing solution. Game engines are essentially platforms on which you can build your code. Developers have already gone through the trouble of implementing low-level functions and making it work on a given platform, it's your job to use these tools to create your game. If this sounds like the APIs I mentioned earlier, it's because these are essentially the same thing, except a game engine uses the platform's APIs to do its job and you use the game engine's APIs to do what you need.

Since the coding is at a higher level, you can focus more on your game and less on low-level setup. Though they used to be clunky and have awful performance, engines like Unity show us your mobile platform game doesn't need to have less than stellar graphics. In fact, Unity supports not only iOS and Android, but PC, Mac, Playstation 3, Xbox 360, and Wii. Though it does take a performance hit from being so large and non-native, the developers of game engines work to make their platform faster and sleeker all the time, which serves to make your games look better without you having to put in more effort.

A few negatives to note is although the free version of Unity works on a select few platforms, Unity Pro is a large hike up in price, currently $1500 plus an additional $1500 per platform or $75/month. Also, though the game engine's developers work to make it better all the time, updates may break your existing code or slow it down. Just keep these things in mind as explore this option.

> *Pros:* Great graphics, and you won't have to worry about low level code.
>
> *Cons:* Some performance hits. Not suited for non-game apps. High cost spike when moving away from free version.
>
> *Choose this if:* You are developing a more-complex-than-simple game and want it to be multiplatform.

Titanium

```
var win = Ti.UI.createWindow({
backgroundColor:'red',
title:'Simple Hello World',
url:'main_windows/cleanwindow.js'
});

var l = Ti.UI.createLabel({
    text:'Hello World',
    color:'#888',
    font:{fontSize:20},
});
win.open();
win.add(l);
```

The folks at Appcelerator have come up with a programming platform compatible with both iOS and Android using JavaScript, the same language used with HTML5 (Appcelerator, 2013). By using their platform, you can maintain one set of code which works natively on each supported platform. This feat is accomplished by their use of APIs and the ability to translate JavaScript quickly at runtime. Titanium is also more open than the other development platforms since it's an open source project. Being "open source" means the community can all contribute to the project and are better equipped to solve problems than they would be with a closed-off environment. Although you can't use all the platform-specific functions with Titanium, if you don't need them, then you'll see no difference and have the added bonus of having a multiplatform app.

> **Pros:** *If any performance hits are present, they are very minimal. Apps work as if native on iOS and Android.*
>
> **Cons:** *Cannot use platform-specific functions.*
>
> **Choose this if:** *You have an app up to medium complexity that you want to be multiplatform.*

Going forward

Although I won't talk any more about multiplatform languages, it's not to suggest they're an invalid choice. By all means, if you want a multiplatform app and your idea meets the criteria, start developing on one of those platforms. Though my coding examples may not apply to you, they're still useful for getting a feel for what code looks like, how long it takes, and what goes into it.

What language to work with is only half the story. In order to know what you're developing on and how you're developing it, you need to choose a platform.

Programming Language Compatibility

	Android	iOS	Windows Phone
Java	✓		
Objective-C		✓	
C#			✓
HTML5	✓	✓	✓
Utility	✓	✓	✓
Titanium	✓	✓	

Choosing a Platform

Picking a platform for your app is perhaps one of the most important decisions you will make for your app. Though it may be tempting to just pick one and go with it, if you spend just a few minutes thinking about where you want the app to be released, your available resources, and what you want out of your app, you'll be in far better shape down the road.

Initial Investment

Developing apps is relatively inexpensive. Most software applications to program and test your code are free, but there is still some startup cost associated with becoming an app developer.

Hardware

The kind of computer you have available to you to program with is important. If you already have a machine you'll do your development on, it's important to know what platforms are compatible with it. If you have a Windows PC, you can develop for Android and Windows Phone without any problems. Unfortunately, Apple tries very hard to make it impossible to develop for iOS unless you have a Mac. There are ways around this, including building your own Mac, called a Hackintosh, running a virtual Mac system in software, and using a third party program to compile code without having to use Apple's Xcode system. Generally it's just easier to stick with what you have available. If you have a Mac, iOS is the easiest system to code for, though Apple does have Boot Camp to allow you to easily install Windows on your Mac, so that's another option if you want to develop for Android or Windows Phone.

Another piece of hardware worth thinking about is the phone you currently own. If you've already bought into a particular phone OS, it's not a bad idea to begin developing on its platform. Not only will you be able to debug faster, but you can show your app to people while it's still unreleased and get feedback. For apps designed to provide some function to users, feedback from someone who has never seen it before is invaluable. There's no problem with testing your program in software, but there are some bugs you'll only catch and performance issues you can only observe when you use your app on hardware.

Cost of publishing an app

For the three major platforms, an upfront investment for writing an app is not required, but if you want the app to be published to the online marketplace, you will need to pay a fee. Sometimes, you can't even put the software on a phone you own until you pay this fee. Although the cost is usually reasonable, it is something to be considered, especially if you're not looking to get money out of your app.

Android

- Cost: $25
- Recurrence: N/A

Google charges a one-time fee of $25 dollars to, in their words, "encourage higher quality products on Google Play (ie. less products with SPAM)" (Google, 2014). This fee allows you to publish your app on the marketplace. It costs as much as a nice dinner for one, so if you're willing to forego a trip to your local sushi restaurant or 23 meals at your favorite dollar menu joint, you're in business.

iOS

- Cost: $99
- Recurrence: Yearly

Apple's fees are quite a bit higher than Google's, coming in at $99 for one year of being a developer. After paying this fee, you now have access to Apple's online resources for iOS programming in addition to being able to submit your app for review to be added to the app store. Prior to this, you'll have to rely on external sources for answers to your questions. Although the increased documentation, code examples, and FAQs are worth the price, the point can be argued you can get similar or equivalent knowledge from free sources.

Unlike with Android, iOS requires you to become a full developer in order to put your app on any phone, even if you own it. All iDevices are locked until you pay the developer fee. This crucial fact may turn off budding programmers if they want to make an app just for themselves or try their hand at coding. For the price for a three course dinner for two at a nice steakhouse, you too can be an Apple App developer.

Windows Phone

- Cost: $99
- Recurrence: Yearly

Microsoft has a similar fee structure to Apple's, but with different benefits. Like Apple and Google, you can publish your app to the marketplace after buying in, but interestingly, access to their code library and examples is free, like with Google. You can unlock one Windows Phone to load your app on to for free, but any more requires a paid developer account. This account also allows you to submit your app to the marketplace. Skipping a family meal at your local chain Italian restaurant will grant you the privilege to put your app in the marketplace and more than one phone.

User Base

If you're looking to make money off of your app idea, another great piece of information to help you decide on your platform is the number of potential customers you can look forward to. It's common knowledge Apple and Google have the majority share of the market, but seeing their exact numbers and those of their competitors will aid in our process.

To reduce the scope of this, let's take a look at just one three month period—Q2 of 2013. As of August 2013, according to research firm IDC, the lowdown on the worldwide market share of mobile platforms is as follows (IDC, 2013):

Platform	2Q13 Unit Shipments	2Q13 % Share
Android (Google)	187.4 million units	79.3%
iOS (Apple)	31.2 million units	13.2%
Windows (Microsoft)	8.7 million units	3.7%
BlackBerry	6.8 million units	2.9%
Linux	1.8 million units	0.8%
Symbian (Nokia)	0.5 million units	0.2%
Other	0.1 million units	0.0%

If you're wondering why I'm choosing to include Windows Phone over BlackBerry or Symbian for the rest of this book, it's because of their shrinking market share. In the last two years, Symbian and Blackberry, once mighty platforms, have seen market share loss of double digits whereas Microsoft has continuously increased its presence in the marketplace.

But we're not only developing for smartphones, are we? Tablets are another medium we must consider. The breakdown for the projected worldwide market share on tablets for September 2012 looks like this (IDC, 2013):

Platform	2Q13 Unit Shipments	2Q13 % Share
Android (Google)	28.2 million units	62.6%
iOS (Apple)	14.6 million units	32.5%
Windows (Microsoft)	2.0 million units	4.5%
BlackBerry	0.1 million units	0.3%
Other	0.1 million units	0.2%

So combining these statistics, we wind up with the following table:

Platform	Units	% Share
Android (Google)	215.6 million units	76.6%
iOS (Apple)	45.8 million units	16.3%
Windows (Microsoft)	10.7 million units	3.8%
BlackBerry	6.9 million units	2.5%
Linux	1.8 million units	0.6%
Symbian (Nokia)	0.5 million units	0.2%
Other	0.1 million units	0.0%

Keep in mind, this does not take into account Apple's colossal lead over Android in previous years, but this is an indication of how things are swinging for the future. So not only does Android have the lowest cost to become a developer, but it has a majority market share in the mobile OS space and is still gaining as well. It seems like the clear choice to develop for, right? It's a little premature to decide that, since there are still many more factors to consider.

Paid vs. Free

We'll get to app pricing in a bit, but for now, let's consider how many users will pay for an app. If you release a non-free app, how likely are people to download it on your platform? An August 2012 study by Swiftkey and Pocket Lint shows the gaps between Android and iOS users (data for Windows Phone users is unavailable) (SwiftKey, 2012).

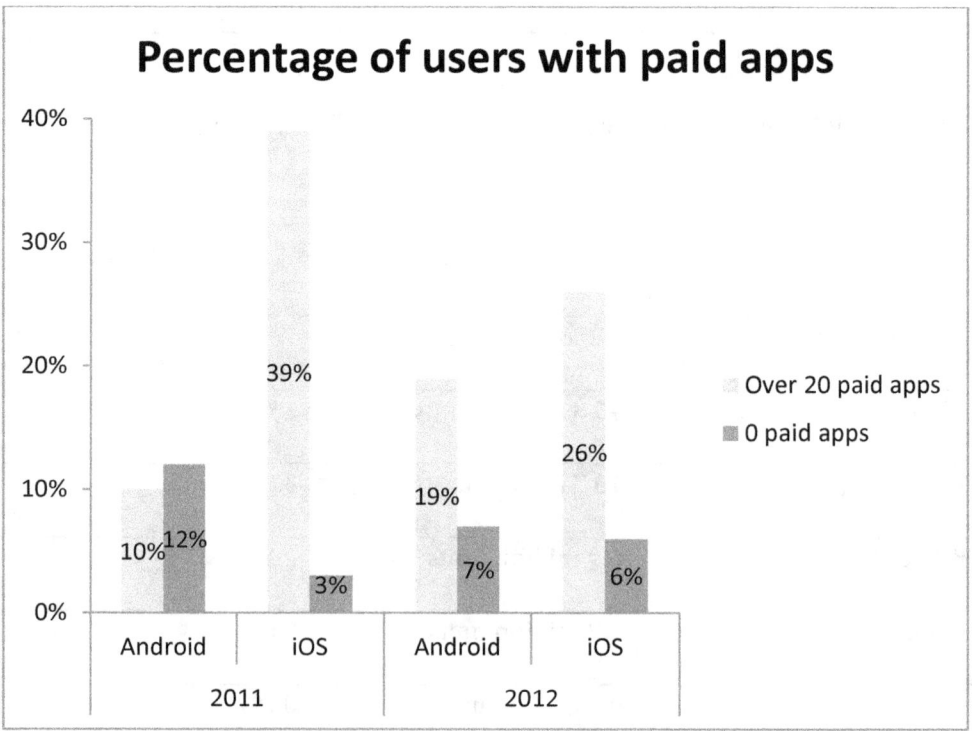

Though the numbers are evening out and coming closer, this data suggests that consumers on Apple's platform are more willing to pay for apps than those on Android.

36

With this new data, assuming the numbers stayed the same in 2013, we can now build a quick table on the available market for your app should you choose to charge for it.

Platform	% with paid apps	Available Market in 2Q13
iOS	94%	43.1 million units
Android	93%	200.5 million units

Although Android users are becoming more willing to pay, iOS users are still more likely to pay for your app. The volumes say Android is the clear victor for market availability, but the percentage of people willing to pay still goes to people with an iOS device, potentially because of the popularity of iTunes gift cards.

The percentage of people with more than 20 paid apps is also telling of the willingness of iOS users to pay for their apps. This data gets even more interesting if you take into consideration the 2Q2013 data analysis done by App Annie on the two platforms showing though Google Play store downloads have risen above iOS app store, app revenue generated through iOS is still 2.3x greater than on Android (App Annie, 2013). This number does not account for in-app advertising, but a study by Opera does.

In a July 2013 report (Opera Software, 2013), Opera concluded iOS took in 49.36% of mobile advertising revenue and Android took 28.08%. Just one year earlier (Opera Software, 2012), the figures were iOS at 61.41% and Android at 24.43%. Though Android is catching up, iOS is still a clear victor for advertisement.

Data for Windows Phone is still scarce, but an August 2013 article in Forbes points to the platform having the highest revenue per download of the three platforms (Louis, 2013). Though this data sounds good on the surface, the small amount of users means it also has the overall lowest revenue.

In the end, if you want to make money off of your app, iOS is the most likely place to generate income. Even if its market share no longer beats Android, the app ecosystem is still far better for developers' wallets than Google's offering. Market trends indicate Android has the potential to one day overtake Apple, but currently, the data spells a very clear story — putting your app on iOS will probably make you more money.

Platform/Solution	Use if
Android	You have a PC and an app idea for which you don't require an upfront fee. The $25 development cost is great for beginners with little cash.
iOS	You have a Mac and an app idea you'd like people to purchase, especially for the tablet space. Still beats Android in revenue generated for developers.
Windows Phone	You have a PC and have an app idea for which you'd like users to pay upfront. The user numbers are small, but growing and the market is not yet mature.

Monetization

Now that you know how many people you could potentially sell to and have a better idea of where you can turn a profit, it's time to figure out exactly how you'll be making money off your idea. If you're only developing an app for personal use, or want to be altruistic and allow your creation to be used for free, there's absolutely nothing wrong with that — you can move on to the next section.

A few monetization paradigms exist in the app world — ad-based, paid, and freemium. Each has its own considerations and example products on which we can take notes.

Ad-based

Example—Draw Something, Angry Birds

Angry Birds is one of the biggest games on any mobile platform and though Draw Something has seen its user base plummet, there was a time in which it was a juggernaut. They're both technically freemium apps, but for the purposes of illustration, let's consider just their ad portions. At one point Draw Something was making $250,000 per day after Apple took its 30% cut (Kafka, 2012). This statistic was from iOS alone. Obviously the ad model can work.

But what kinds of ads work best? Generally, the rule of thumb is: the more attention the ad draws, the higher paying it is. So, for example, a simple banner ad at the bottom of your app will make less money than a full page, app-pausing ad or one pushing notifications to the user's phone. The decision on how intrusive you'll allow your ads to be is completely up to you, but keep in mind users tend to dislike more intrusive ads.

Another consideration to keep in mind is once an app has set up certain expectations for its ad model, if the model is changed to be more intrusive it generally doesn't sit well with the audience. From personal experience, I changed the ads on my app from small banner ads to be full page ads requiring user interaction before the app could be used. The resulting negative feedback and complaints made me switch back soon after.

Ads also introduce a security risk in that some ad providers may not check their ads for potentially malicious code. Smartphones are exploding in numbers, making them a very lucrative platform for malware and extortion practices. In order to keep yourself and your users protected, research the security of your ad provider before integrating their services.

> **Pros:** *Your app is free to users, meaning a wider potential audience. Each new install means more potential income.*
>
> **Cons:** *Ads can reduce battery life. No money made per install. Some ads are intrusive to users.*
>
> **Choose this if:** *Your app is either too simple to warrant being paid for, or you can sacrifice short term, per-customer profits for a long term, passive income.*

Paid

Example—Infinity Blade

Paid apps are exactly what they sound like—the customer pays an upfront fee for your app. Deciding whether or not your app fits this payment model depends on a few things. Do you think its desirability warrants an upfront fee? Is it a killer game nobody has ever seen, or simply an improvement of an existing piece of software? Either way, a user has to feel like the fee was worth the product. Another metric to determine whether the paid route is right for you is whether or not you want to integrate ads. They can distract the user, break immersion in games, and sometimes introduce security risks, so if you don't want to deal with that, paid may be a good route. If your app fits this profile, the next thing you'll need to determine is a price.

Time and money spent producing the app isn't always a good indicator of how much to charge, but it's a place to start. Figure out how long it would take to either make back your initial investment or pay yourself for your time with a given sales price. Then weigh this dollar amount against how many people you think would pay for an app of similar functionality. A good place to start asking for potential customers is with your friends and family, but asking social media outlets like Reddit, Facebook, or Twitter will also yield more varied, honest results for who wants your app.

Something to keep in mind when polling people is that not everyone has your best interests at heart. If someone sees your great idea but is more skilled than you, they may beat you to the punch. If you believe this to be an issue, you can keep your feedback pool to only those you trust and require NDAs for those you don't. You may also consider patenting your idea, though the process usually takes months and $900 if you're doing it yourself, thousands if using a patent lawyer (USPTO, 2013). This preemptive action requires a significant investment you may not be willing to make, so exercise discretion with your ideas.

The next consideration you should make is the price of similar apps. To start with, compile a list of the top three most successful, similar apps and average their price. You can then compare this to the number you came up with earlier and use them for your baseline. They're not hard limits, but users want to feel they've gotten their money's worth and if your competitors offer something similar for cheaper, users will generally feel regretful for their purchase. Haven't you regretted buying something and only using it a few times? Perhaps that Ab Lounger? This feeling of buyer's remorse is something you want your users to avoid, especially if you plan on releasing more products. Charge a reasonable amount of money based off how useful it is to the customer and how it compares to similar apps.

Basically if it's just a soundboard-type application, maybe don't charge five dollars for it.

> **Pros:** *You're paid per download and have control over pricing. No ad integration.*
>
> **Cons:** *Potentially less downloads and slimmer audience. Higher user expectations. Competition may dictate price.*
>
> **Choose this if:** *Your app is complex and you don't want to implement ads.*

Freemium

Example—Tiny Tower, Candy Crush Saga

The freemium model is a strange beast, and one that is evolving rapidly. The idea behind it is to give the app away for free, but charge for upgrades. For instance in Tiny Tower, you can upgrade your tower more quickly by purchasing upgrades. And in Candy Crush, you can buy more lives or different power ups to help you through the game. Offering an incentive to pay money but keeping the game itself free is a great way to appeal to a large audience while still allowing for some form of direct payment. This model also opens up an avenue for passive income and as of December 2013, it's reported to be the majority money maker for app developers is from freemium sales with statistics as high as 90% of revenue coming from in-app purchases (Fox, 2013).

The freemium model has many different implementations revolving around how your money can affect games. In some, you can buy cosmetic upgrades with no effect on gameplay, but rather how the it looks. Others like Tiny Tower will help you in the game, but not so much as to be unfair. And yet others give you upgrades designed to help you out immensely. Each model is no less valid than the other, but users generally dislike feeling like they must pay to win.

This model doesn't just apply to games. Some business apps will only unlock certain features if you pay a premium. For example, an alarm clock app could have you pay for the ability to play a song from your library instead of the standard collection of sounds. Picking which features to charge for may be difficult, but try putting yourself in your customers' shoes. Make sure the additional features you're charging for are not ones the user will feel cheated by not having.

As always, when you're the party handling money, you need to make sure you're taking proper security measures. Since you're the one who's coding the purchase transactions, you'll need to ensure all transactions are secure. If you're handling the card information, you have to ensure you're following security standards like PCI-DSS for compliance and safety. If you're implementing a third party vendor's APIs to keep track of billing, be aware of their compliances and security measures as well before selecting them to use for yourself.

> **Pros:** *Control over monetization. More potential revenue per user. Can add to user purchase options for more potential revenue.*
>
> **Cons:** *Upgrade offerings should be worthwhile, but also not make the user feel cheated. Must build store infrastructure and deal with security.*
>
> **Choose this if:** *Your app is complex and has features that can easily be added and enabled.*

Combining

Monetization methods are not mutually exclusive. The freemium model can be used in conjuncture with the ad model, but generally not with paid. People start to get a bit miffed if they pay to use an app but have to pay again to unlock the app's full potential.

A quick, easy method of having multiple releases of the same app with different revenue streams is to have two separate apps, one paid and one with ads. This combination serves to apply to a wider audience and give a preview to the customer of what the app is, but gives them the option to pretty it up with a little cash. Angry Birds in particular has a free version supported by ads and a premium paid version with the ads removed. Freemium would take the two apps and slam them together, allowing the user to purchase the right to disable ads within the app.

Even if you don't think users will pay to have ads disabled, it can't hurt to try. The worst case scenario is nobody buys it and users continue downloading the free version. The only reason I never did it with the app you'll see later is I had already integrated ads into it and did not want to take the twenty minutes it would have taken to create a paid version. Let that be a lesson — laziness doesn't pay.

Using these models in conjunction can produce very lucrative apps with a satisfied user base.

Certainty of Release

When making an app for release, the process can take some time depending on the platform for which you are developing. Even after the app is completely finished, it can take weeks before your app is ever on the market, if it's even seen at all. Yes, the possibility exists you'll spend a few months working on an app only to have it rejected and never see the light of day. Let me explain why.

Android is a mostly open platform and allows any app on their market. If you've made an app, you can upload it directly to the market and people can start downloading it immediately. The upside for developers is that your apps will never be barred from release. Though they may be taken down later if flagged for malware or doing something to violate a provider's Terms of Service, you're guaranteed to be able to upload your app. The downside to the freedom of release, combined with the lower fee to become an Android developer, is market saturation. Big ones, small ones, free ones, dumb ones, new ones, old ones, you name it, Android probably already has it. For developers, the large population means you'll feel more pressure to stand out from the noise to be successful, but the cost is low enough to justify the risk. Failing on this platform isn't as significant as it is with other platforms.

iOS and WP7/8, however, are closed platforms. Being part of a closed platform means much higher quality control from the standpoint of Apple and Microsoft. When an app is submitted to either market, it is first reviewed by the parent company for metrics of quality and to verify it is working. If it passes the quality testing and adheres to the guidelines, it will be published to the store.

That's how it should work, anyway.

Unfortunately, apps are reviewed by people in some cases and people are not perfect. This system allows for the possibility of good apps being rejected by employees based on personal taste. Microsoft is better about this than Apple as their quality assurance measures revolve mostly around the app working, whereas Apple also determines if the app meets a certain standard of quality. In both cases, however, it can lead to your months of toiling way, staring into The Forever that is your code, being flushed down the toilet as it's never released. Most times, the company will provide feedback on how to correct or make the app better for resubmission. If you've implemented your ads incorrectly, overwritten some variable, or did an insufficient amount of testing for multiple platforms, both platform providers will let you know. For iOS, you may get an email saying your app adds too little value to the market and are told to make it better. It's a risk you take developing for either iOS or Windows Phone, but if you want to break into those markets, it's necessary.

Conclusions

So we now have a ton of information to chew through and determine a plan of action. The next section is about my personal experience with the proprietary languages of each of the major three platforms. If you're going with a multiplatform language, you can skip this part, though you'll be missing out on platform specific information you might find useful later.

Case Studies

In this section, we'll examine the source code for my app on all three major platforms and the process it took to get there.

App Idea

My father is no technological savant, but he's doing his best to keep up with the times. In early August 2011, he purchased his first smartphone — a Motorola Droid II. Try as he might, he could not find a specific app and called me to ask how to find it. He described the app from a popular Geico commercial at the time where you press the screen and an animated dog would say "Yeah dawg!" He thought it would be hilarious to torture my mother with. I looked in the Android Marketplace but couldn't find anything. When I told him, he said what got me started on my app writing journey.

"You're a programmer, why don't you just make it?"

Huh, y'know I never thought about that, I considered.

"I'll get back to you when it's done," I told him.

There was no reason I couldn't do it. I had an Android phone, a PC, and cursory knowledge of programming. This task answered most of the questions I've posed in the previous chapters since he wanted it for his Android phone and I didn't deem it complex enough to warrant charging for it. Since then, my app enjoyed over 100k total installs on Android in its lifetime and I have ported it to both Windows Phone and iOS. Since Android started my app development career, why don't we start there?

I'll structure each platform by giving a brief overview of the project scope and length, then show my source code, followed by how much time was taken by each of the four major sections – Layout, Code, Ads, and Submission. The Layout section is about making the app's appearance and user interactions, in this case, consisting of displaying the Yeah Dawg animation and ads. The Code section is about the code it takes to make the app function – playing the sound and triggering the animation. The Ads section will be how I integrated ads into the finished product, and the Submission section will be the challenges I faced when submitting my app to the marketplace.

For all following code examples, you can download my entire project file from http://gettingstartedwithapps.com/downloads/

> If you want to get an idea for how to design your user interface, you can use what's called paper prototyping to show off your ideas to people. Essentially, you just draw what the interface should look like on paper and present it to people to gauge their reactions. In fact, you can download an app for Android and iOS called POP - Prototyping on Paper that will allow you to create links on top of the images that will go to other images, effectively turning your pictures into a dummy app. For an example on this, check out my example café app at
>
> http://pop.gettingstartedwithapps.com/

Android

Time frame: 2.5 full days

From installing the software to its initial submission to the Android Marketplace, Yeah Dawg's development cycle only took 2.5 days. The first 1.5 days saw the completion of the app's code, audio, and art resources with another day to put ads in place.

Compatible with: All Android devices from 1.6 up

Time breakdown per section:

Code

I won't go into details on what I did for the images and audio, but I created them in Paint.NET and Audacity respectively. It took approximately two hours to get everything finalized.

One unexpected choice I had to make with Android was with which versions my app should be compatible. Google has put out numerous revisions of Android, adding new code functionality each time. If you choose a higher revision number, chances are it won't work on older revisions of the OS. In order to make my app apply to the most phones I could, I picked version 1.6, which is the earliest version that supported all the tools I needed for Yeah Dawg.

As it turns out, animation is a difficult subject to learn for beginners on a new platform. Luckily, Yeah Dawg only consists of two static images for animation. Even so, it's rather difficult to approach the subject knowing nothing about the language's implementation. Fortunately, Google has an entire library dedicated to animation, so a quick search on the internet came up with many resources on how to implement it. In my case, I created an XML object called an Animation List, and then specify the frames in the animation and how long they stay on screen. Once defined, I simply accessed it from the main code and set it to play.

Next, I needed to play the audio I've recorded at the same time. The SoundPool object loads the clip and prepares it to play. It's generally used for smaller audio like sound effects in games, which is perfect for this app. I loaded up the sound file and every time the screen is pressed, I played the audio file along with the animation.

A nice feature I stumbled into with this code is it will restart any time you press the screen, but the audio and video will continue trying to play and overlap itself. It makes for fun times when you press it as fast as possible. This coding practice is not recommended for larger applications as it eats more resources the more times you press it, but for something small like Yeah Dawg, it's a fun little feature.

All of this coding took about eight hours of research into the APIs I needed and trial and error to get them to work.

Layout

Now I had to lay out the **views** where I wanted them, as seen in main.xml. After a few hours of searching, I finally realized I wanted to have a view for the animation and below it, the view for ad space and have the two dynamically align themselves no matter the screen size. This feature is done with the Relative Layout XML object and use of layout align and gravity options.

Due to unfamiliarity with XML and layouts in general, it took time to learn what I was supposed to be doing and how to get my views working with one another. Getting the layout to compile and look how I needed it took another four or so hours.

Ads

The final piece of the Yeah Dawg puzzle was advertisements. After getting the layout to work appropriately, another day was spent coding and testing the **adspace** code. The ad code needed to be downloaded separately from the ad provider I chose, AdMob, instead of being integrated into the IDE like with Microsoft and Apple. Though this took relatively little time, it did add some complexity and challenges I didn't face with other platforms.

I was having problems getting test ads to work due to screen layout problems, but I finally fixed the problem by changing how I declared and implemented the AdView space in the layout. Instead of creating it in the code, I instead declared it in the XML. In layman's terms, I made it so the ads are always part of my app instead of trying to insert them after it starts.

Getting ads to work in Yeah Dawg took approximately eight hours of Googling and workarounds.

Submission

Uploading Yeah Dawg took very little time. I clicked a few buttons in the environment, created a key for the app, and had a secure file exported to my computer. From there, I uploaded it to the Android Marketplace, added some preview screenshots and a description and it was up. Twenty five dollars and ten minutes of my time was all it took to have it available to people. This process was by far the easiest and most pleasant of the three.

Relevant code:

Yeahdawg.java (code file)

In Java, everything is done with classes. The class we're creating to handle everything for Yeah Dawg needs to handle touch input and create objects, hence implementing OnTouchListener and extending Activity. Extending from Activity means our new class can do all of the things the pre-defined Activity class can do.

```
public class yeahdawg extends Activity implements
OnTouchListener{
```

Next, we set up the variables we'll need to manipulate. Our AnimationDrawable will handle the animation, SoundPool will play the sound we need, and AssetManager will fetch our files for us. The two Rects will be used later to resize the image to the screen's size. Display will get us the size of the screen.

```
        AnimationDrawable mainanimation;
        SoundPool soundPool;
        int yeahDawgSound=-1;
        AssetManager assetManager;
        Rect orig = new Rect();
        Rect finished = new Rect();
        Display display;
```

The onCreate method will run whenever this class is created, which will be as soon as the app runs in our case. This instance of onCreate will override any of the onCreate methods of classes we inherit from, namely Activity.

```
        @Override
        public void onCreate(Bundle savedInstanceState){
```

Here, we request access to the full screen feature, allowing us to make the Android status bar go away.

```
                requestWindowFeature(Window.FEATURE_NO_TITLE);
```

In this line, we set the application to be full screen.

```
getWindow().setFlags(WindowManager.LayoutParams.FLAG_FULLSCREEN,
                WindowManager.LayoutParams.FLAG_FULLSCREEN);
```

Since we've overridden the onCreate method for Activity, it needs to be called manually with the Bundle previously passed in. This call will ensure everything for our Activity is set up correctly.

```
super.onCreate(savedInstanceState);
```

We set the current view to be the layout we defined in main.xml

```
setContentView(R.layout.main);
```

These lines will load a new ad into the AdView we set up in main.xml

```
        AdView adview =
(AdView)this.findViewById(R.id.adView);
        adview.loadAd(new AdRequest());
```

We set our display variable equal to the default display, allowing us to get the size of the display.

```
display= getWindowManager().getDefaultDisplay();
```

These lines set the ImageView we specified in main.xml to our animation. The ImageView then gets set up to listen for touch input. Whenever the animation is touched, a method defined later will be called.

```
        ImageView mainimage = (ImageView)
findViewById(R.id.mainanim);
        mainimage.setBackgroundResource(R.anim.mainanim);
        mainimage.setOnTouchListener((OnTouchListener)this);
```

Here, we resize the animation to fit the full screen. We do this by resizing the height according to the ratio of the width of our image to the width of the screen.

Since the actual face is in the middle of the image, resizing should not distort the image.

```
            mainanimation = (AnimationDrawable)
        mainimage.getBackground();
            orig=mainanimation.getBounds();
            int height= (int)display.getHeight() *
                    (orig.right/display.getWidth());

        finished.set(0,display.getHeight(),display.getWidth(),hei
    ght);
            mainanimation.setBounds(finished);
```

We set the volume control to apply to our sounds and get a new SoundPool to load our sound into.

```
            setVolumeControlStream(AudioManager.STREAM_MUSIC);

            soundPool = new
    SoundPool(20,AudioManager.STREAM_MUSIC,0);
```

Try statements attempt to do an action and if an error occurs, the code in the catch statement is run. So in our try statement, we have our asset manager trying to get our audio file. If it could not get the audio, an error is captured in our log file. If the sound was successfully retrieved, it's loaded into our SoundPool, ready to be played. Also, yeahDawgSound, a variable I used to make sure the audio was loaded, will be set to something other than its initialized value of -1.

```
            try{
                    //load sound
                    assetManager = getAssets();
                    AssetFileDescriptor descriptor =
                    assetManager.openFd("yeahdawgsound.ogg");
                    yeahDawgSound =
                    soundPool.load(descriptor,1);
            } catch (IOException e){
                    Log.d(null,"Couldn't load sound effect
 from asset, " + e.getMessage());
            }
                                    }
```

The onTouch method will run anytime the ImageView containing our animation is touched.

```
    @Override
    public boolean onTouch(View v, MotionEvent event){
```

This code only runs when you pick your finger up from the screen. All other inputs are ignored.

```
            if(event.getAction() == MotionEvent.ACTION_UP){
```

If the sound was loaded properly, yeahDawgSound should now be something other than -1. If it is, we tell the animation to run and the SoundPool to play the sound. After it's over, we return true to indicate the process happened successfully.

```
            if(yeahDawgSound!=-1){
                //start animation and play sound
                mainanimation.run();
                soundPool.play(yeahDawgSound, 1, 1, 0, 0, 1);
            }
        }
        return true;
    }
}
```

Main.xml (file containing layout information and ad data)

Everything inside Main.xml is contained within a RelativeLayout, a type of Layout that allows us to define our views in relation to one another. This view is vertical and takes up the whole screen. It does not display anything on its own, but rather acts as a container for Views that display information or images.

```xml
<?xml version="1.0" encoding="utf-8"?>
<RelativeLayout
xmlns:android="http://schemas.android.com/apk/res/android"
xmlns:ads="http://schemas.android.com/apk/lib/com.google.ads"
android:id="@+id/mainLayout"
android:orientation="vertical"
android:layout_width="fill_parent"
android:layout_height="fill_parent"
>
```

This ImageView will contain our animation later. It's defined to fill its parent, which means it will adjust its size once we have an ad to display in the adview below.

```xml
<ImageView android:id="@+id/mainanim"
android:layout_above="@+id/adView"
android:layout_width="fill_parent"
android:layout_height="fill_parent"
android:gravity="center"
android:layout_centerHorizontal="true"
/>
```

This adview has my adUnitId replaced for privacy reasons. It specifies to create a banner ad below its parent, which in our case is the ImageView above. The gravity attribute being set to bottom means it will stay on the bottom of the screen.

```xml
<com.google.ads.AdView          android:id="@+id/adView"
android:layout_width="wrap_content"
android:layout_height="wrap_content"
ads:adUnitId="xxxxxxxxxxxxxxx"
ads:adSize="BANNER"
ads:loadAdOnCreate="true"
android:visibility="visible"
android:layout_alignParentBottom="true"
android:layout_gravity="bottom"
android:layout_weight="1"
/></RelativeLayout>
```

MainAnim.xml: (File containing the definition of our animation)

This xml defines the animation for our program. Yeahdawgonebig shows the dog with his mouth closed, and yeahdawgtwobig has the mouth open, so the durations are timed to have his mouth opened when talking over our audio. These times were arrived at through trial and error, but fit pretty well.

```xml
<?xml version="1.0" encoding="utf-8"?>
<animation-list
xmlns:android="http://schemas.android.com/apk/res/android"
android:oneshot="true">
<item android:drawable="@drawable/yeahdawgonebig"
android:duration="150" />
<item android:drawable="@drawable/yeahdawgtwobig"
android:duration="125" />
<item android:drawable="@drawable/yeahdawgonebig"
android:duration="150" />
<item android:drawable="@drawable/yeahdawgtwobig"
android:duration="150" />
<item android:drawable="@drawable/yeahdawgonebig"
android:duration="150" />
</animation-list>
```

Platform wrap-up:

I went from having no code to a fully tested and working, albeit simple, application on the Marketplace in two and a half days. Just a weekend and a little time after work on Monday. I found plenty of resources online giving example code for the animation, audio playing, and ad implementation. Anytime I had a problem, I had a window open with search results for whatever I was working on alongside the open source Android SDK documentation. Though Google does a reasonably good job of showing how its functions work, I found very little helpful example code applying to my project. Luckily, places like Stack Overflow had more than enough people asking questions similar to my own so my questions were answered quickly.

Pros	Cons
• Code was relatively straightforward • Software was free • Tons of example code easily found • Low cost of becoming a developer	• Layouts were a pain to get working • Separate code module needed to be installed and integrated into the project for ads • Multiple hardware vendors and software updates means you must carefully choose which version of the platform to develop for and code appropriately

iOS

Time frame: 6 full days + 3 weeks

Once Xcode was up and working, it took me approximately six days to finish Yeah Dawg. Three days were spent writing the code and getting it functional with the iPhone and an additional three were spent making the code work with iPad, enabling ads, and prepping for app store submission. Three weeks were then spent waiting for approval from the app store.

Compatible with: All iOS devices

Time breakdown per section:

Code

The code for this project was quite daunting. As a programmer, I've had experience with scripting and object oriented languages before, but Objective-C is completely alien to me. The syntax, procedure of running, and code are all foreign. Since I came into this language entrenched in object-oriented coding methodologies, it was difficult to switch gears and learn how to use this language.

The resources available to learn how to program Objective-C are abundant and Apple's own documentation was exceptionally helpful in this project. After paying my developer fee, I got access to a library full of example code and helpful suggestions to aid me. I still found myself turning to the internet for help, but would keep the documentation open to peruse it if I had forgotten how to implement something.

I spent three days making Yeah Dawg talk and move in code, investing most of my time into the animation framework.

Layout

The layout for this project was mostly straightforward and without hassle. I just create the views and had them added to the layout, then they were displayed exactly as I hoped. This process may sound complicated, but it was as easy as dragging and dropping an icon from the tool bar into the window. I had some trouble with dimensions between different resolutions at first, but quickly solved those by having multiple resolution versions of the images and having iOS select which was appropriate to use based on the screen resolution.

One area of difficulty was setting icons up. Because of the quickly growing amount of different resolutions and products that run iOS to support, different icons with different resolutions with different background must be made for each one. I had to remake the same icons four times and give them all specific filenames since I wanted to support all the resolutions iOS supported. It was a pain, especially since I had to specify far fewer for Android and Windows Phone and their filenames could be anything.

The layout should have taken a short amount of time, but a full day was spent making the icons work with multiple platforms.

Ads

I had a problem with iPhone to iPad compatibility and it had to do with the ads. On iPhone, the ads would display beautifully, exactly as they were supposed to, but the iPad ads would never come up. After far too much time playing with numbers, searching, looking in documentation, and head scratching, I finally fixed it with the help of a forum post and some trial and error.

For another full day, I spent far too much time researching ad implementation before being successful.

Submission

The submission process for iOS was by far the most needlessly complicated process I encountered. Two days were spent trying to solve the mystery of submission. Though I had guides and help from people on forums, I still found myself with confusion about what licenses I needed, different certificates I had to generate, and what I needed to do to convert my application from development to release. With the other two platforms, it was far less complicated and never took more than an hour to have something ready to upload. For iOS, it took a little more than a day.

Additionally, this is the only platform on which Yeah Dawg was never published. I submitted my app for approval but was denied on grounds of it not adding enough value to the App Store. Whether that's true or not, the statement shows how tightly Apple controls the quality of apps they allow on their platform. They have chosen to have more quality control over programs sold in their store and as a result, your app can be rejected based on their preference, subject material of your app, or its usefulness. This fact also means if your app idea was deemed not high quality enough for the iOS platform, you've just paid Apple a nonrefundable $99 to have them tell you "Sorry, try again."

Relevant code:

YeahDawgViewController.m (Where all pertinent code lives)

The import statement for the .h file associates our file full of code with a header file. The header file is then used by pre-built app framework in order to access this code. I also import the AudioToolbox so we can use its functions to play sound later.

```objc
#import "YeahDawgViewController.h"

#import <AudioToolbox/AudioToolbox.h>

@implementation YeahDawgViewController

@synthesize bannerIsVisible;
```

This block of code runs to make sure the banner ads I installed have loaded correctly. If they did, the ad is set to be visible if it was previously not.

```objc
-(void)bannerViewDidLoadAd:(ADBannerView *)banner
{
    if(!self.bannerIsVisible)
    {
        [UIView beginAnimations:@"animatedAdBannerOn"
        context:NULL];
        banner.frame = CGRectOffset(banner.frame,0,-
        banner.frame.size.height);
        [UIView commitAnimations];
        self.bannerIsVisible = YES;
    }
}
```

If the banner ad failed to load, it is set to invisible if it wasn't already.

```objc
-(void)bannerView:(ADBannerView *)banner
didFailToReceiveAdWithError:(NSError *)error
{
        if(self.bannerIsVisible)
        {
                [UIView beginAnimations:@"animatedAdBannerOn"
                context:NULL];
                banner.frame =
                CGRectOffset(banner.frame,0,banner.frame.size.he
                ight);
                [UIView commitAnimations];
                self.bannerIsVisible = NO;
        }
}
```

This code is run when the user interacts with the ad. If you to grant them the ability to interact with the ad (and you generally do), you'll want to set shouldExecuteAction to be YES.

```objc
-(BOOL)bannerViewActionShouldBegin:(ADBannerView *)banner
willLeaveApplication:(BOOL)willLeave
{
        NSLog(@"Banner view is beginning an ad action");
        BOOL shouldExecuteAction = YES;
        if(!willLeave && shouldExecuteAction)
        {
        }
        return shouldExecuteAction;
}
```

If the banner ad is finished loading and I wanted it to do something, this is where I'd put the code. Luckily, I didn't need to do anything, but this function is required for submission and approval from the App Store.

```objc
-(void)bannerViewActionDidFinish:(ADBannerView *)banner
{
}
```

The block of code contained in this function is run when the app starts, so here's where we set up everything we need.

```objc
- (void)viewDidLoad {
    [super viewDidLoad];
```

The animation is defined here with static images. yeahDawgAnim is an animation object I defined in a different file, but here is where I'm setting all of its properties. I couldn't quite figure out how to get the static images to have their own duration time on the screen with the way I decided to code this, so instead, I padded the animation images with duplicates to make the time line up correctly. Below, you can see I set the animation duration to be 1.2 seconds, the length of the audio file, and with the image padding in the animation images, Yeah Dawg's mouth opens at the correct times.

```objc
yeahDawgAnim.animationImages = [NSArray arrayWithObjects:
[UIImage imageNamed:@"yeahdawgonebig.png"],
[UIImage imageNamed:@"yeahdawgonebig.png"],
[UIImage imageNamed:@"yeahdawgonebig.png"],
[UIImage imageNamed:@"yeahdawgtwobig.png"],
[UIImage imageNamed:@"yeahdawgtwobig.png"],
[UIImage imageNamed:@"yeahdawgtwobig.png"],
[UIImage imageNamed:@"yeahdawgonebig.png"],
[UIImage imageNamed:@"yeahdawgtwobig.png"],
[UIImage imageNamed:@"yeahdawgtwobig.png"],
[UIImage imageNamed:@"yeahdawgtwobig.png"],
[UIImage imageNamed:@"yeahdawgonebig.png"],
[UIImage imageNamed:@"yeahdawgonebig.png"],nil];

yeahDawgAnim.animationDuration = 1.2;
yeahDawgAnim.animationRepeatCount = 1;
```

To display this animation to the screen, we add it to views being displayed with addSubview.

```objc
[self.view addSubview:yeahDawgAnim];
```

Here, I set up the adview, allocating its size and orientation. I also set the banner to be invisible after adding it to the current view. It will make itself visible when an ad is loaded because I then called the viewDidLoad function defined earlier.

```objc
    adView = [[ADBannerView alloc] initWithFrame:CGRectZero];
    adView.requiredContentSizeIdentifiers = [NSSet
    setWithObject: ADBannerContentSizeIdentifierPortrait];
    adView.currentContentSizeIdentifier =
    ADBannerContentSizeIdentifierPortrait;

    CGRect adFrame = adView.frame;
    adFrame.origin.y = self.view.frame.size.height;
    adView.frame = adFrame;

    [self.view addSubview:adView];
    adView.delegate=self;
    self.bannerIsVisible=NO;
    [super viewDidLoad];
}
```

This block of code runs every time the app is touched, so here's where we'll define when and how to play the sound and start the animation.

```objc
- (void)touchesBegan:(NSSet *)touches withEvent:(UIEvent *)event
{
```

First, I get the sound and load it up using AudioServices.

```objc
    NSURL *soundURL = [[NSBundle mainBundle]
    URLForResource:@"yeahdawgsound" withExtension:@"mp3"];
    SystemSoundID soundID;
    AudioServicesCreateSystemSoundID((CFURLRef)soundURL,
    &soundID);
```

Then I play the sound.

```objc
    AudioServicesPlaySystemSound(soundID);
```

If the animation has already started, I stop it before starting it again. This bit of code is to make sure I'm not trying to start an animation that's already playing, which would cause an error. It functions a bit like the Android app in how every touch plays a new Yeah Dawg, but instead of playing on top of one another, the currently running one stops and the new one starts.

```
        if ([yeahDawgAnim isAnimating]) {
            [yeahDawgAnim stopAnimating];
        }
        [yeahDawgAnim startAnimating];
}

//deallocate memory appropriately
- (void)dealloc{
        [super dealloc];
        adView.delegate=nil;
        [adView release];
        [yeahDawgAnim release];
}

@end
```

Platform Wrap-up:

What sticks out most to me about iOS was how difficult it was to bring the app to release. Between the small annoyances like having to remake and rename images multiple times and the complicated process just to upload my app for review, it was much harder than the same procedure on Android or Windows Phone. Everything up to the app's submission was roughly as difficult as it was on other platforms and required similar debug and research efforts. The platform's age meant I could more easily find helpful code examples or people with similar problems, which was a huge advantage over a newer platform like Windows Phone. Overall everything leading up to prepping the app for submission was on par with Android despite having no prior experience with the language, but the confusing mess after was such a hassle, it left a bad taste in my mouth.

Pros

- Documentation was the most helpful of all the platforms
- Layout was easy to use
- Ads were simple to integrate for one platform

Cons

- Supporting multiple resolutions was a chore
- Ads didn't work immediately for different resolutions and devices
- Icons were a pain to implement

Windows Phone

Time Frame: 3 days + 2 weeks

Nearly three days were spent doing the layout and getting it to work properly. The code and ad implementation took less than an hour combined. The longest part of the process was waiting for approval, which took two weeks.

Compatible with: Windows Phone 7, Windows Phone 8, and relatively easy to port to Windows 8

Time breakdown per section:

Code

Coding this app took approximately thirty minutes. As you'll see later, most of the work is in the layout. The code section checks to see if the animation is currently playing. If it is, the animation is prevented from being started again. This coding decision, which differs from the app's functionality on Android and iOS, was done because the animation and audio file could not be overlapped in Windows Phone without error. To prevent overlap, I coded a simple checker to set a variable to true when the animation starts and false when it ends.

Coding this very simple function and making sure it worked took approximately half an hour.

Layout

The bulk of my effort was spent on the layout. After approximately two days of coding and experimenting with different animation techniques, I finally settled on having an animated button. Previous ideas ranged from a strict Canvas with user interaction integrated into it to a custom transparent button to cover the Canvas and trigger the animation starting. Eventually, after much trial and error, I got the actual button to do the animating for me. After specifying where my **Storyboard**, the container for my animation, was supposed to be stored and drawing to, all I needed to do was specify the frame for animation. This bit was also tricky because the timing never seemed to work out right. Whether it was due to my poor understanding of the structure or lack of friendliness of the available tools, I couldn't seem to get it to work for a couple of days.

Also of note is despite my best Google-Fu, I couldn't find a page to describe animating a button for WP7/8. Thus, the failed ideas I discussed earlier were tried, until I happened upon a solution myself. Since this platform is so new, it was quite difficult finding coding examples or helpful forum posts to alleviate my issues. The Microsoft documentation is extensive and provides helpful example code, but like with Android, not much of it answered my specific question. It wasn't necessarily a shortcoming of the documentation, as this is quite a specific application, but I couldn't put the pieces together without my own trial and error. It didn't help that that Visual Studio and XAML were giving me less than helpful messages about my code. This process resulted in a day in which if I hadn't broken the animation, I had messed up the dimensions on the button, or the sound wouldn't play, or my XAML was deformed. It took a non-trivial amount of time to get working, which was a shift from Android and iOS where any layout problems I had took very little time.

Arranging the layout and making it all work took very near three days due to poor debug messages and very little guidance for animated buttons.

Ads

Ad units are a place where Microsoft did exceptionally well. To implement them in code, I simply dragged and dropped. The code was automatically implemented without any hassle. I spent maybe five minutes looking through documentation on how to implement it, but after the initial setup, I had no troubles with it for the rest of my development cycle.

Ad integration took five minutes maximum.

Submission

Platform submission for Windows Phone took quite a bit longer than with Android, but a little less than iOS. Exporting my program and uploading preview images, icons and the like took a reasonable amount of time, but because Microsoft must review the app before allowing it on to the store, the time before being published was increased significantly. They run checkers to do quality assurance and make sure it's not malicious before approving it to the store, and these security checks can take time. On average, users in 2012 saw anywhere between 7 and 13 days for approval (Various, 2013). My submission was on the high side of this spectrum, coming in at 2 weeks.

Something else to keep in mind is this app will only be applicable for Windows Phone. In order to distribute to the app store for Windows 8 on tablets and PCs, you'll need to recode a bit, recompile the code, and have a separate submission. The submission is subjected to a similar, but not identical, process and you'll have to be reviewed again.

The overall process was simple; just make sure to not plan your launch party for the day of submission. We don't want guests showing up to have you say, "Oh well see, now someone's going to review it and try it out on a system. No, not today, sometime in a week or two. But it's still mildly exciting!" The party would be a horrible, time-wasting faux pas.

The waiting time between my app being completed and it appearing in the store was about two and a half weeks.

Relevant code:

MainPage.XAML (Where the layout is determined, and in this program's case, the animation and audio)

Here, we're defining the dimensions of both the app and the Canvas within the app. The Canvas is our drawable area, allowing us to use it for our animation. For this particular app, having it be as large as the screen is appropriate.

```
shell:SystemTray.IsVisible="True" d:DesignHeight="768"
d:DesignWidth="480">
    <Canvas xmlns="http://schemas.microsoft.com/client/2007"
    xmlns:x="http://schemas.microsoft.com/winfx/2006/xaml"
        Width="480" Height="768"
             x:Name="YDCanvas">
```

Once the Canvas has been defined, we set its background element to the first image in the Yeah Dawg animation so before anything is pressed, the user sees the first image.

```
        <Canvas.Background>
            <ImageBrush ImageSource="yeahdawgonebig.png" Stretch="Fill"/>
        </Canvas.Background>
```

Now we create a button within the Canvas. This button will contain all of the elements of our animation and handle the user input.

```
            <Button x:Name="button1" Margin="0" Click="Button_Click"
    Opacity="0" BorderThickness="0" Height="768" Width="480">
            <Button.Resources>
```

The high level animation framework I chose for Windows Phone is the Storyboard construct. Here, I've defined its name and duration.

```xml
<Storyboard x:Name="YeahDawgStoryboard"
    Duration="0:0:1.175">
```

Within the storyboard, we use ObjectAnimationUsingKeyFrames as the animation input. As the name implies, this animation is done using key frames, meaning it flips between static images at set intervals. Many types of animation are supported by Windows Phone, but since we only have two images in this app, using key frame animation is the most appropriate way to do it. We also specify the Canvas it'll be using and what part of the Storyboard it will be redrawing.

```xml
<ObjectAnimationUsingKeyFrames
    BeginTime="0"
    Storyboard.TargetName="YDCanvas"
    Storyboard.TargetProperty="Background">
```

Each DiscreteObjectKeyFrame defines what image should appear and how long it should stay on screen. They are defined linearly, meaning the images appear in the order they're specified in the code from top to bottom. The KeyTime values shown here were approximations based on playing the audio file multiple times and tweaking the values. Though I could have looked at the actual duration of the words in the audio file, this seemed to work well enough and took less time.

```xml
                        <DiscreteObjectKeyFrame
KeyTime="0:0:0.3">
                            <DiscreteObjectKeyFrame.Value>
                                <ImageBrush
ImageSource="yeahdawgonebig.png" />
                            </DiscreteObjectKeyFrame.Value>
                        </DiscreteObjectKeyFrame>
                        <DiscreteObjectKeyFrame
KeyTime="0:0:0.45">
                            <DiscreteObjectKeyFrame.Value>
                                <ImageBrush
ImageSource="yeahdawgtwobig.png" />
                            </DiscreteObjectKeyFrame.Value>
                        </DiscreteObjectKeyFrame>
                        <DiscreteObjectKeyFrame
KeyTime="0:0:0.6">
                            <DiscreteObjectKeyFrame.Value>
                                <ImageBrush
ImageSource="yeahdawgonebig.png" />
                            </DiscreteObjectKeyFrame.Value>
                        </DiscreteObjectKeyFrame>
                        <DiscreteObjectKeyFrame
KeyTime="0:0:0.75">
                            <DiscreteObjectKeyFrame.Value>
                                <ImageBrush
ImageSource="yeahdawgtwobig.png" />
                            </DiscreteObjectKeyFrame.Value>
                        </DiscreteObjectKeyFrame>
                        <DiscreteObjectKeyFrame
KeyTime="0:0:0.9">
                            <DiscreteObjectKeyFrame.Value>
                                <ImageBrush
ImageSource="yeahdawgonebig.png" />
                            </DiscreteObjectKeyFrame.Value>
                        </DiscreteObjectKeyFrame>
                    </ObjectAnimationUsingKeyFrames>
                </Storyboard>
            </Button.Resources>
```

Triggers are a type of Interaction, meaning a way in which the user can interact with your app. Triggers are defined by their start condition and actions, in this case a Click (or in the case of an app touch) and playing our audio file.

```
            <i:Interaction.Triggers>
                <i:EventTrigger EventName="Click">
                    <im:PlaySoundAction 
Source="/yeahdawgsound.mp3" Volume="1"/>
                </i:EventTrigger>
            </i:Interaction.Triggers>

        </Button>
```

This incredibly small piece of code defines how our Advertising code works. We essentially define the ApplicationId and AdUnitId, both values we get from the ad network so it knows what size ads it should be serving and to validate that it's serving them to the right app, as well as the height and width of the ads and the location of the top of the Canvas. With all of this information, ads are served reliably to our app without any further instantiation.

```
            <Microsoft_Advertising_Mobile_UI:AdControl 
ApplicationId="XXXXXXXXXXXXXX" 
AdUnitId="XXXXXXXX" Height="80" Width="480" Canvas.Top="688"/>
    </Canvas>
```

MainPage.xaml.cs (Where the C# code is implemented to play the animation and audio)

This is the entire code section of this app (quite small compared to the rest of the platforms). The class structure in this app is akin to that of Java in that MainPage is a part of PhoneApplicationPage.

```
public partial class MainPage : PhoneApplicationPage
    {
```

I keep track of whether or not the app has been clicked or not using this variable of type bool for Boolean (a variable type named after 19th century mathematician George Boole). These variables can only take on the value of true or false, making them perfect for telling whether something happened or not. In this case, it starts as false and is only made true when the button is clicked.

```
        private bool isAnimating = false;
```

This code runs at the start of the app. It initializes the components within the app and sets up the background framework needed to run. Here, I also say a function below (onCompleted) should run when my Storyboard has stopped being animated.

```
        public MainPage()
        {
            InitializeComponent();
            YeahDawgStoryboard.Completed += new EventHandler(onCompleted);
```

This function runs every time the button is clicked. If our Boolean variable is set to true, meaning the animation is still going, I exit before doing anything. However, if it's false, meaning the animation has either completed or hasn't started yet, the animation starts.

```csharp
        private void Button_Click(object sender, RoutedEventArgs e)
        {
            if (isAnimating)
                return;

            isAnimating = true;
            YeahDawgStoryboard.Begin();
        }
```

When the animation is complete, our Boolean is set back to false, allowing the user to press it again.

```csharp
        void onCompleted(object sender, EventArgs e)
        {
            isAnimating = false;
        }
    }
```

Platform wrap-up:

Windows Phone is a young platform. Programmers are trying to feel it out and Microsoft is still looking to improve it. As the platform becomes more popular, more resources will become available and the learning curve will be less daunting. At the moment, however, it's a bit like trying to find a venue your friend told you about vaguely with no GPS, directions, map, or street signs. Just wander aimlessly down some streets, talk to some strangers who are just as lost as you, and eventually you'll find your way.

Pros
- Ads are easy to integrate
- New platform means more improvements on the way
- Huge documentation library
- Free software comes with tutorials, companion programs, and more that are useful

Cons
- Young platform means less third party documentation and FAQs
- Proprietary XAML can get confusing and daunting
- Not very beginner friendly

Time Spent Breakdown

	Android	iOS	Windows Phone
Code	8 hrs	3 days	30 mins
Layout	4 hrs	1 day	3 days
Ads	8 hrs	1 day	5 mins
Submission	10 mins	1 day + 3 weeks	1 hr + 2 weeks

Personal Preference

The differences between the platforms boiled down to where the most time was spent. For Android, it was mostly coding and getting the layout to work, though the time spent on both was rather reasonable. Windows Phone saw a longer time spent making the layout work appropriately and learning the syntax of the language due to less information being available. iOS had a major problem with its long submission process, compatibility issues between different devices and screen sizes, and strict submission process. Though they all had their drawbacks, Android was the clear winner in my case as the submission process was a breeze, multiple screens were supported simply, and most of my time was spent actually coding instead of figuring out how to trick the software into doing what it was I wanted it to do. For my money, Android was the appropriate choice to begin programming with a PC and an Android phone. Windows Phone took a close second with iOS bringing up the rear. This experience doesn't mean iOS is terrible, as all three experiences were relatively painless and had me up and working within a week. I simply had the least frustration with Android as a platform than any others.

Conclusion

So now you're ready to go. With a plan in mind, it's time to get your first "How to Program" book and start making things yourself. I hope this guide will assist you in hitting the ground running and make your development experience more pleasant. Whether you're an iOS developer who wants to make a single platform banking app, or a Windows Phone developer who is hopping in on the ground floor with a killer gas price tracker idea, or an Android developer whose dad wants them to help in annoying their mother, we're all programmers developing for the same sector with a common goal—to see our work in the hands of people. I can't begin to explain how gratifying it feels to see a friend using your app, even if it is just to annoy you. Even if your download numbers are small, it's also incredible knowing someone to whom you have no connection is using your app.

Whether you're buying a book, learning from a teacher, or subjecting yourself to trial by fire with the internet as your sidekick, keep your motivation steady through the discouragement and tough times so you can make something we can all use.

Now go forth and create! If you'd like more information, guidelines, and up to date info on platforms, visit this book's website at http://www.gettingstartedwithapps.com.

Glossary

Adspace – The portion of the screen dedicated to displaying ads

App – As it applies to mobile operating systems, apps are any application run on the operating system, generally downloaded from a centralized store or marketplace.

Application Programming Interfaces – Predefined functions or structures to accomplish certain tasks in code. When referring to a mobile OS, APIs include things like setOnTouchListener for Android or the Storyboard structure for Windows Phone.

Canvas – In the context of apps, a Canvas is a drawable area, generally defined as a rectangle. Within this area, you can draw to individual pixels, load and display images, or manipulate anything within the Canvas as you see fit. This flexibility makes it a perfect candidate for games as you'll be redrawing the images anywhere from 30 to 60 times per second.

Documentation – The written descriptions of the code in question. The documentation is where you'll turn to if you need questions answered about code you're using. If you write your own app, you'll want to write your own documentation too. I can't tell you how many times I've written a piece of code and come back after a few days and had no idea what it does because I didn't document it properly.

Haptic Feedback – Tactile feedback that uses the sense of touch to interact with users. Typically, cell phones use vibration as haptic feedback.

Integrated Development Environment – A program used to write, design, debug, and release code.

Native – Native, in the context of apps, refers to languages that run on the system without a third party software being needed. Examples of this are Java on

Android, Objective-C on iOS and C# on Windows Phone. HTML5 would not be a native language since it requires a web browser to be interpreted.

Object – In code, objects are constructs programmers use to keep track of information. They typically represent real world items and contain data relevant to those items. For example, a Calendar object may contain the days of the week, what day today is, and the dates for the rest of the year.

Open Source – Open Source refers to when a program's source code, the code that makes up the program, is freely available to the public.

Performance – When talking about code or software, performance generally refers to how quickly a given piece of software will work.

Storyboard – For Windows Phone, a Storyboard refers to an animation construct in which you can define an animation, its duration, and its size. Within your code, you can start, pause, and stop the animation with pre-defined commands.

User Experience – The look, feel, and experience you want your app to have with a user. User experience decisions include colors, button shapes, layouts, fonts, and audio cues.

User Interface – What the user sees and how they interact with your program. User interfaces should ideally be intuitive, easy to use, and visually appealing.

Views – In the context of apps, views represent different displays within the app. For instance, for an alarm clock app, you may have an alarm view to show details of the alarm, list view to list all alarms, and menu view to display options.

References

App Annie. (2013, July 21). *App Annie Index – Market Q2 2013: Google Play Exceeds iOS App Store in App Downloads by 10% in Q2 2013.* Retrieved from App Annie: http://blog.appannie.com/app-annie-index-market-q2-2013/

Appcelerator. (2013, December 5). *Titanium mobile application development.* Retrieved from Appcelerator: http://www.appcelerator.com/titanium/

Appthority. (2013, February). *App report.* Retrieved from Appthority: https://www.appthority.com/appreport.pdf

Fox, Z. (2013, December 19). *Freemium Is the Most Profitable Pricing Strategy for Apps.* Retrieved from Mashable: http://mashable.com/2013/12/19/paid-vs-free-apps/

Google. (2014, January 2). *Developer Registration.* Retrieved from Android Developer Help: https://support.google.com/googleplay/android-developer/answer/113468?hl=en

IDC. (2013, August 7). *Apple cedes market share in smartphone operating system market as Android surges and Windows Phone gains, according to IDC.* Retrieved from IDC: http://www.idc.com/getdoc.jsp?containerId=prUS24257413

IDC. (2013, August 5). *Tablet shipments slow in the second quarter as vendors look to capitalize on a strong second half of 2013, according to IDC.* Retrieved from IDC: http://www.idc.com/getdoc.jsp?containerId=prUS24253413

Kafka, P. (2012, March 12). *Zynga just bought OMGPOP for $200 Million.* Retrieved from All Things D: http://allthingsd.com/20120321/looks-like-zynga-just-bought-omgpop-for-200-million/

Louis, T. (2013, August 10). *How much do average apps make?* Retrieved from Forbes: http://www.forbes.com/sites/tristanlouis/2013/08/10/how-much-do-average-apps-make/

Opera Software. (2012, July). *The state of mobile advertising, Q2 2012.* Retrieved from Opera Software: http://www.operasoftware.com/archive/sma/2012/q2/index.html

Opera Software. (2013, July 23). *Apple leads mobile OS in monetization and traffic, but Samsung keeps Android in close competition.* Retrieved from Opera Software: http://www.operasoftware.com/press/releases/mobile/2013-07-23

SwiftKey. (2012, August 29). *Android catching up with iPhone on paid apps.* Retrieved from SwiftKey: http://www.swiftkey.net/android-catching-up-with-iphone-on-paid-apps

USPTO. (2013, December 5). *Current fee schedule.* Retrieved from USPTO: http://www.uspto.gov/web/offices/ac/qs/ope/fee031913.htm

Various. (2013, December 5). *What is the current average time for approval?* Retrieved from Windows Dev Center Forum: http://social.msdn.microsoft.com/Forums/windowsapps/en-US/b7a64d84-a54f-4b3f-a953-14555505ca9e/what-is-the-current-average-time-for-approval?forum=windowsstore

www.ingramcontent.com/pod-product-compliance
Lightning Source LLC
Chambersburg PA
CBHW081836170526
45167CB00007B/2823